TWO MONTHS IN ITALY

An Architect's Diary

TWO MONTHS IN ITALY

An Architect's Diary

PAUL OSTERGAARD

ISBN: 979-8-218-25992-1
Imprint: Paul Ostergaard, FAIA

Photographs and sketches by Paul Ostergaard.
Book design by Susann Reimann.

First printing edition 2023.

Beginning in Turin in late April, I took a counterclockwise path down the west coast of Italy, around Sicily, and up the Adriatic coast, finishing in Verona in late June.

TABLE OF CONTENTS

INTRODUCTION

After a long career as an architect and urban designer, I found time to publish this record of a formative adventure I had many years ago. In late spring of 1978, I began a two-month journey of Italy. I had recently won the Stewardson Prize, a design competition among architects studying in Pennsylvania. The prize was a travel stipend that I used to explore Italy. After graduating from Carnegie Mellon University, I worked at Urban Design Associates to save up enough additional money to make a nice go of it in Europe.

As a student, I spent many hours studying landmark buildings and urban environments created over the centuries and dreamed of seeing these places firsthand. Carnegie Mellon had a wonderful faculty of architectural historians, including Howard Saalman, Patricia Waddy, Franklin Toker, and Robert Taylor. I relied on extensive notes from their courses to plot a path through Italy. I consulted with Raymond Gindroz, a partner at UDA, to fill in my itinerary with important stops.

I traveled by myself, armed with two sketchbooks, a bottle of ink and a dip pen, a 35mm camera, my diary book, my itinerary, and a guidebook. With a rail pass and Italy's extensive rail network, travel was easy. This book combines my drawings, photographs, and simple daily notes into an illustrated travel diary. My text is often shorthand, largely unedited.

⟨ PAUL OSTERGAARD, FAIA ⟩

TURIN

APRIL 28

Took the Paris metro to Gare Lyon and caught the train to Turin. The train passed through the Alps. The views were spectacular. It passed along a large lake somewhere in southern France and then up through the mountains. The train went through several tunnels, one almost 5 miles long. Vistas were constantly shifting from one side to the other. At the border, we could tell we were entering Italy. Instead of a straight conductor's signal whistle, it was a sexier whistle with two fingers and a couple of shouts. The radios started blaring after the Italians got on the train, and kids were hanging out the windows. In general, things got livelier.

Turin is a prosperous, elegant city. It is the only Italian city of its type, laid out on a grid. The major streets (Via Roma, for example) are lined with arcades two or three stories high that are very wide, giving the impression of civic grandness. The buildings are five or six-story high structures, often grayish in color although sometimes of painted stucco. The city is full of grand palaces and beautiful facades. The continuity of the neon signs was very pleasing.

Arcade on the Via Roma

Cloudy, rain. Saw Piazza San Carlo. An interesting gateway was formed by two churches. Cars go between the churches, pedestrians around.

Saw Guarini's Palazzo Carignano, now the Accademia delle Scienze with a facade beautifully articulated in brick. The curving facade of the palace seems to embrace the whole square in front of it.

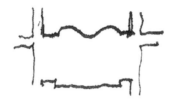

Palazzo Carignano, 17th Century, Guarini

4

Piazza San Carlo

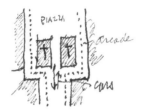

Facade of the Palazzo Madama, 18th Century, Juvarra

Saw the church of S. Lorenzo and Cappella della Sacra Sindone. Sindone's space was very dark, being made of dark marble, yet it worked well. It contrasted with the light coming from above in the cupola and added to the mystique. The entrance was very dramatic. The steps seemed to resist your approach until you entered the circular vestibule, and then they draw you in. It is one of the few triangular spaces I've ever been in. Did a drawing of the dome sitting on the freezing floor and was observed by a class of young school kids.

Saw Palazzo Madama. There was an interesting exhibit of literature by Russian dissidents. Had a pizza, cake, and red wine for dinner.

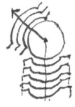

S. Lorenzo, 17th Century, Guarini

Cappella della Sindone, 17th Century, Guarini

Saw the collections at the Palazzo dell'Accademia delle Scienze and Palazzo Carignano. Could only peer into the grand sala of the Palazzo Carignano. It was redone to be an assembly hall for government and has been left in that state for the museum. It was not what I had expected, but it is a nice reuse for an old palace. The problem is that Guarini's fabulous sequence of entry using his main stairs and halls is not used now. That's too bad. You can walk up the steps to the main level but can't go into the sala or museum from there.

Rain prevented me from seeing the Superga by Filippo Juvarra up in the hills. The river Po was really flowing, and there was an interesting-looking convent on top of a small hill just across the river.

Everything was quiet in Turin this rainy Sunday until around three, when people started walking up and down the arcaded boulevards, window shopping, going to movies, etc. Many were very well dressed. One gets the definite impression that Turin is a wealthy city. Suddenly the city turned into a tremendous victory celebration for an Italian soccer team that won the gold cup or something. The streets filled up with cars blaring their horns, people waving flags, lots of spectators, TV camera crews, and crowds of kids. It was quite unexpected on this cold dismal day. Had antipasto, pizza, beer, and fruit for dinner. I am very impressed with Italian food. The pastries are delicious, and the selection of things in the stores and restaurants is of continual interest.

Courtyard of the Palazzo Carignano, 17th Century, Guarini

<MILANO>

MILAN

MAY 1

Caught the 9:30 train to Milan. Passed through very flat land. Some farm fields were flooded, the water levels being controlled by dikes. I assume these were for growing rice, although I am not sure. Arrived at the Milan Centrale railroad station. It's huge to the point of being severe. Found a hotel room nearby. Walked into the city. It's a national labor holiday, and practically everything, including the trams, were closed. Saw the famous Galleria. In the evening, around 5:30 to 6:00, many Italian gentlemen gathered at the end of the Galleria near the Duomo, standing very close together, discussing issues of the day. Some were very animated in their speech, waving their arms gesturing loudly. This reminded me of Saul Steinberg's sketch of this very thing in this same setting. Maybe the architecture ennobles the user to the point of such direct and obvious display.

Central dome of Galleria Vittorio Emanuele II, 19th Century

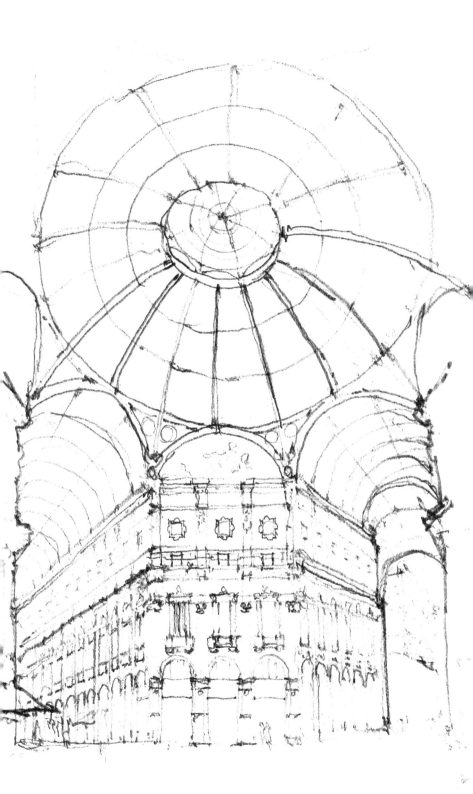

Galleria Vittorio Emanuele II,
19th Century

Cathedral Facade, 14th–20th Century

Piazza del Duomo

I climbed up on the top of the cathedral, around the spires and weird buttresses, and saw much of Milan from there. Only church towers, modern skyscrapers, and antennas pop above a uniform building height. The city seems sort of flat from up there.

The museum at the Castello was closed, but people could still pass through the courtyards from one end to the other. This passage provides a marvelous transition between the urban fabric of the city and natural park setting, and it was a heavily used route on this holiday. It takes people from one of Milan's major shopping streets anchored at one end by the duomo square, through the castle domain to the park, with the other end of the park expressed by a triumphal arch clearly visible on axis with the path.

Promenading through Castello Sforzesco

Saw some of the museum collections at the Castello. It makes a nice museum. Went to Santa Maria delle Grazie and saw the "Last Supper" by Leonardo da Vinci. It is in bad shape but is being worked on. There are some nice courtyards by Bramante. The church dome and crossing are also by Bramante. Outside was a fascinating play of volumes and openings, rich in color from the stone and terracotta. Inside, the proportions and subdued articulation was very pleasing. Bramante's work respects the human scale. Interesting vaulting and superimposed articulation with his circle motif are seen in the choir. Went to Ospedale Maggiore and saw many courtyards within the complex.

Refectory of the Convent of Santa Maria delle Grazie,
15th Century, Bramante

Ospedale Maggiore, 15th Century

Santa Maria delle Grazie Cloister, Bramante

Went to Saint Ambrogio and was very impressed. Wonderful court in front of the basilica. The facade with loggias blends into the court arcade. More is done here with brick and stone than most any place I recall. The nave elevation doesn't have much elaborate carving, but the interesting use of stone, brick, and plaster give it a fine richness. Saw the remains of St. Ambrogio and another guy. Weird, sort of gruesome, but fascinating. At least this church still has its saints (relics). The tallest tower is leaning a little.

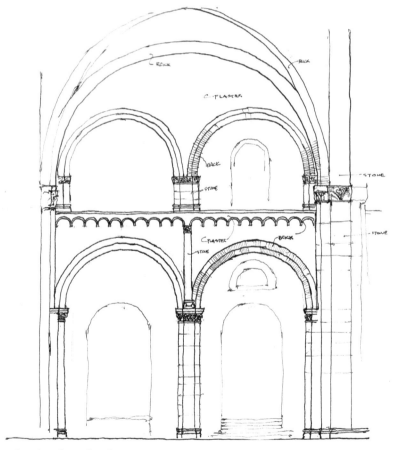

Nave elevation of S. Ambrogio

Exterior elevation of S. Ambrogio, 9th–11th Century

Entrance court of S. Ambrogio, 9th–11th Century

Saw San Satiro by Bramante. The perspective of the false choir on the wall really works if you enter through the main entrance. I was surprised to see that I had entered the transept and that the nave bent on around but there was no choir. The perspective tricked me further. Articulation on the nave barrel vaults is smooth except in the perspective where it is molded with coffers, increasing its effectiveness. The church was dark. The piers and articulation were monumental in their forms but quite small. The church seems bigger in photographs. Very human in scale again, almost miniature.

S. Satiro, 15th Century, Bramante

Castello Sforzesco, 15th Century

Saw a large collection of musical instruments, pottery, and other objects at the Castello Sforza. Walked through Parco Sempione where many people were lounging about on this beautiful day. It's a very nice park.

Walked down to St. Eustorgio to photograph and draw it. Again like St. Ambrogio, marvelous things have been done with brick and stone. There is a very interesting Renaissance chapel behind the choir.

Saw a collection of art at the Biblioteca Ambrosiana including da Vinci sketches and then walked to the Palazzo E. Museo di Brera.

Nave Elevation, S. Eustorgio, 4th–16th Century

S. Eustorgio, 4th–16th Century

Parco Sempione

VIGEVANO

I took the train from Milan to Vigevano to see the Piazza Ducale by Bramante. So much was done with the construction of a continuous arcaded facade. A harmonious space was created uniting circulation and objects. Views along paths were framed, and entrances created to buildings and streets. Paving created different spaces and zones in the piazza. Bicycles rode along the smooth surfaces, which happened to be placed on direct routes. Approaches to the square were carefully designed. Views of the square were framed by the arcades crossing the approaches, and in many places the two major towers were visible, popping into view or seen towering above in the distance. Photographic sequences can best describe it. The town seemed reasonably prosperous. Cars were not allowed in the square.

Piazza Ducale, 15th Century, Bramante

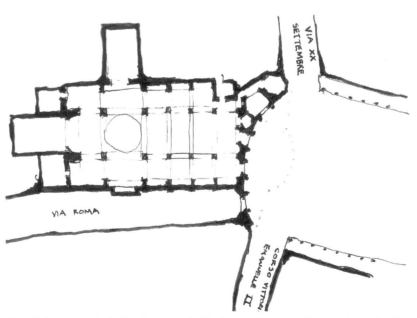

Plan of Vigevano Cathedral in Piazza Ducale. The baroque facade has four portals, one leading into a baptistery, one into the nave, one into a side aisle, and one the Via Roma.

ABBIATEGRASSO

Went to Abbiategrasso and saw a huge portico and intimate courtyard done by Bramante. The terracotta work glowed in the late afternoon sun, red against blue sky and green grass. Fresco and stone added variation and color. Just outside the courtyard were simple narrow streets, tan in color, providing a nice contrast to the rich courtyard and creating a nice spatial experience. Had pasta, roast beef, potatoes, and an apple for dinner + aqua minerale, and lemon ice cream.

S. Maria Nuova Courtyard, 15th Century, Bramante

S. Maria Nuova Facade, 15th Century, Bramante

GENOVA

Took the train to Genova, but rain prevented me from seeing most of what I had planned. However, I saw the Palazzo Reale. It is very palazzo-like in the front along the street but becomes very villa-like once you pass through the entrance. The geography makes it such a very dense urban situation with a clear view of the port and the Gulf of Genoa. Across the street at the Palazzo D. Universita, a different situation occurs. This palace is built into the hillside. Entering from the bottom, it has a typical courtyard, although terraced levels and cascades of stairs modify it from the typical. The stairs lead to what is practically a roof garden but still within the palace domain.

The Palazzo Reale had a fine exhibit about the restoration of paintings and buildings being done in Genova. The drawings of the buildings were beautiful. I found a very interesting market street, Via del Campo, running parallel between Via Balbi and Via Gramsci. It was very narrow but was full of the life of Genova. It is out of the way and can't be seen well. I found it by walking down one of the many footpaths between buildings and streets terraced on the hillside. I saw a little square and was attracted to it. When I got there, I heard lots of noise coming from somewhere further down the hill and found this street packed with markets, noise, and the smell of roasting coffee.

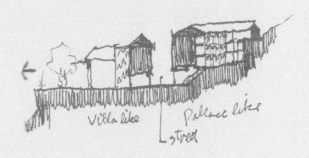

Villa like | Pallace like

street

Palazzo D. Universita

Palazzo Reale, 17th Century

Palazzo D. Universita

MANTOVA

Took the train to Mantova. Found an albergo across the street from the RR station for 4,800 lire a night. The first thing I saw was the architect Giulio Romano's house. I couldn't get in, but the facade was clearly visible and well-kept. A powerful facade with two stories, the lower level is expressed as a wall and the upper level as an arcade. The horizontal band separating the two bends up to form a pediment over the entrance. The view from down the street is where I think the facade has its most power and easily stands out from the others because of the horizontals. Saw Alberti's Church of S. Sebastian.

S. Sebastiano, 15th Century, Alberti

Saw the Palazzo D. Te by Romano and loved it. The sculpted facades are powerful in the sunlight. In the garden facade he plays with walls and columns in the "Palladian motif" around the openings. The garden loggia is very comfortable. Layers of columns provide a nice sense of enclosure within this outside-covered space. I could sit there for a long time. Rooms are handled in an interesting manner. The walls are smooth and plain up to 7 to 8 feet in height, and then elaborate wall-ceiling surface treatment is employed. The ceilings are a real joy to see, and the variety is delightful. The parts of the walls that can be touched and easily decorated are left smooth for the user, while the part of the room that is not functional gains its use from its beautifully designed treatment. The loggia was separated from the garden by a "dry moat," and a bridge, reminiscent of Roman bridges, connects the two.

Palazzo del Te, 16th Century, Romano

Loggia of the Palazzo del Te

S. Andrea is Alberti's masterpiece. The facade fronts a small square and contributes to the fun of the main pedestrian streets and shoppers traffic flow. It was dark inside and the chapels were almost totally dark. His treatment of them using the alternating circle and rectangle is nice. In the evenings, people promenade along a route connecting the major piazzas, Piazza D. Erbe, Sordello, and Marconi.

Basilica of S. Andrea, Mantova, 15th Century, Alberti

Palazzo Ducale, 14th–17th Century

MAY 7

Visited the Palazzo Ducale. It's a multitude of courtyards and rooms built during various periods. Beautiful wooden ceilings are seen in the older ones. The miniature rooms for the court dwarfs were fabulous. High enough to stand in, they were complete with niches, vaulting of all types, domes, nice door frames, etc. The labyrinth of rooms included halls, stairs sized to dwarfs, a chapel, etc. It was like walking through a model. It would be a kid's paradise.

Lazy afternoon. Did some sketching and soaked up some sun. Had a Sunday afternoon dinner in the Piazza Erbe, which included macaroni, some sort of baked fowl, fruit, and red wine. In the evening, I walked through the town one last time and looked more closely at the Palazzo Broletto. This medieval palace has a very nice staircase in a small courtyard. Large arches span across the passages around the palace courts. That evening one could easily let your imagination wonder how these courts were used and what happened in them years ago.

BOLOGNA

Left Mantova on a crowded local train and arrived at Bologna. On the way, I could see the arcade going from the city to St. Luca. Found a hotel and sent off a package of stuff to home. Hope it gets there. I had a hard time communicating with the postal workers. The package was supposed to be specially wrapped, but out of frustration they took it the way it was.

Saw Bologna. Beautiful day. Climbed all the way to the top of the tallest campanile located in Piazza Porta Ravegnana. Got a marvelous view of the city from up there. Next to that campanile is one that leans probably just as much as the one at Pisa. Walked along the famous arcades. Nice medieval palaces around Piazza Maggiore. One has a small courtyard one story above ground level that looks across the forecourt and out into the piazza. It is overlooked by the palace's campanile. Many food stands in streets behind the major boulevards that connect the two major piazzas. Vast selection of fresh fruit, vegetables, fish, meat, etc.

Piazza Maggiore, Bologna

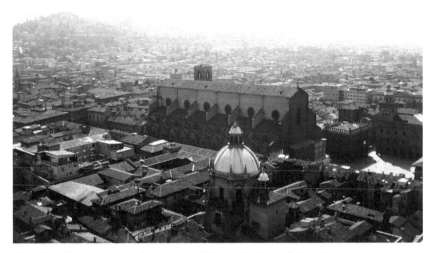

View of Basilica San Petronio from the Asinelli Tower in Piazza di Porta Ravegnana

View of the Piazza di Porta Ravegnana and adjacent tower from the top of the Asinelli Tower

PARMA

Took the train to Parma. It was the nicest Italian train I had been on yet with new extremely quiet coaches. The baptistery truly is one of the finest buildings I have ever seen. Internal and external facades are beautifully handled, well-proportioned, and articulation is controlled. The shape of the baptistery is powerful. Whole square is very nice with buildings of a light pinkish stone and brick. The nave elevation in the church was frescoed, providing a pleasant alternative to other Romanesque churches. Architectural elements including cornices were painted on the flat wall. Human figures sometimes overlap the painted cornices creating subtle contradictions in the nature of the surface vs. object relationship, a three-dimensional play. Visited a gallery in the massive almost inhuman Pilotta Palace.

Parma Cathedral, 11th–12th Century

Parma Baptistery, 12th–14th Century

Interior of the Baptistery

MODENA

Then took the train to Modena. The Romanesque duomo was worth the trip. The massive treatment of interior nave elevations, thick walls on columns, brickwork, and elevated choir with a visible crypt level reminds me of St. Zeno's in Verona. The campanile is very nice and is connected to the church by arches. The long cathedral facade facing the piazza is articulated similarly to adjacent building arcades in its repetition of surface elements. Nice portico there.

Noticed many people gathering in the town piazza. Saw communist flags and Christian Democratic flags as well with posters and signs. The crowd grew until the square was packed, then people started speaking. I thought it was a political rally until later that night when I was eating dinner with Soreo from Jesi, did I discover it was to pay respect to Aldo Moro, who was found assassinated earlier this day in Milan. Soreo was a nice Italian kid, spoke limited English, but we were able to communicate a little. Exchanged addresses.

Modena Cathedral, 11th–14th Century

Arcade in the Piazza Grande

Piazza Grande

<FIRENZE>

FLORENCE

Raining in Bologna. Saw the major art museum in the city, full of local Renaissance work nicely displayed. Medieval and early Renaissance painting is beginning to grow on me. I found this exhibit to be fascinating and could have spent hours there, but the museum closed at 10:00 am as well as most every other place in Bologna, to pay respect to Moro. I am still trying to get more information on this tragedy but can't. All the Herald Tribunes have been sold out. They hadn't arrived in Bologna yet when I left at 12:00 noon.

The train to Florence was through rugged countryside, very beautiful but with many new buildings scarring the landscape. Saw a terrible derailment. A train had fallen off the track and down a steep embankment. The rail cars I saw had been badly smashed, and the undercarriages were scattered about. Got a room in Pensione Mary.

Took a lightning walk through Florence. Beautiful weather, clear sky, and warm. I approached S. Lorenzo with keen anticipation and entered the church. Marveled at the nave and decided to visit Brunelleschi's chapel first, so I walked over to it (I knew exactly where it was from my studies of it), stepped inside, and saw that it was filled with scaffolding. Disgusted, I walked over to Michaelangelo's chapel but couldn't enter that way. I had to go around to the outside entrance. By the time I got there, it was closed. Oh well.

Excited by the Florentine facade work at S. Maria Novella and the Duomo (green and white stonework). Have much to see.

S. Maria Novella, 15th Century

Duomo, 13th–15th Century

Cathedral Complex including the Baptistery, Campanile and Cathedral

View from the top of the Cathedral Dome

Started on my way to S. Lorenzo and walked through a major market next to the church. Visited the Medici chapels again. Michaelangelo's is such a total complete controlled world. The architecture and sculpture create a complete setting; a struggling dynamic balance is achieved by using architecture that is sculpted and varied by two colors. The walls are packed with these elements leaving not much room for any additions. There is a certain beauty of economy in his use of just two colors and sculptural play within a set of rules. Plaster and white stone are used side by side, but even though there is a slight variation in color, they are not noticed until you touch them up close.

The courtyard of the church was pleasant. The entrance to the library was on the second level. He packed a monumental stair in such a small space leading to a small door. Double columns struggle with beautifully framed niches. His framing of things in three dimensions is like an intricate puzzle. The elements are easily seen and understood but are put together in a fascinating way.

Exterior of the New Sacristy by Michelangelo

S. Lorenzo, 15th Century, Brunelleschi

*Palazzo Medici–Riccardi,
15th Century, Bartolomeo*

Saw Palazzo Medici-Riccardi. Couldn't get to the main sala, but the chapel was nice, although it didn't have any windows. The double courtyard-garden combination was pleasant, sort of a frontyard-backyard relationship. Saw the Palazzos Pazzi and Strozzi. Strozzi was covered completely by scaffolding. Florentine palaces have similar characteristics; three levels with varying degrees of surface rustication, arched windows, and a heavy cornice.

Palazzo Medici-Riccardi Courtyard

Palazzo Pazzi, 15th Century, Maiano

Palazzo Pazzi Courtyard

View from the Uffizi of the Cortile, Palazzo Vecchio, and the Cathedral dome in the distance

Studied the Uffizi space a bit. The cornice really helps to create the line of the space, demarcated against the sky. Sculptures at one end seen from the other end of the space appear almost as a point, although separated enough to see each one. As you walk through the space the duomo's dome comes into view, then disappears. The angle of the Palazzo Vecchio is enough to see the facade, and the campanile is in the center of the view. When you enter the Piazza della Signoria, the sculptures separate and become individuals against the solid uniform walls of the Palazzo Vecchio.

The Church of Ora S. Michaele was interesting. It was originally a double loggia market building. The upper floors were used for storage of grain, etc. in case of famine or disaster. A double nave was created, two altars, one with special painting, the other standard. The church was sponsored by the trades, so tabernacles dedicated to each one is displayed on piers around the facades.

View of the Piazza della Signoria

Cortile of the Uffizi, 16th Century, Vasari

Foundling Home, 15th Century, Brunellschi

The Orsanmichele was interesting. Originally a loggia market building, it was transformed into a church. The upper floors were used for storage of grain and offices. A double nave was created, two altars, one with a special painting, the other standard. The church was sponsored by the trades and beautiful tabernacles are dedicated to each one displayed on piers around the facades.

Brunelleschi's Foundling Home, early classical building in Florence, simple efficient elements, clean, and nice. Now part of it is an art gallery.

Orsanmichele, 13th–14th Century

Visited S. Croce and the Pazzi Chapel. S. Croce has a beautiful timbered ceiling. The Pazzi Chapel by Brunelleschi is in a nice pastoral courtyard with lots of grass, pine trees and sky. It is a pleasant chapel with nice terra cotta work, gray stone, and white walls. Assembly of the parts is masterful. Visited National Museum and saw lots of wonderful little objects including pots from Urbino. Objects like the ones on display are things you could stare at for a long time.

Porch of the Pazzi Chapel, 15th Century, Brunelleschi

Ceiling of the Basilica of S. Croce, 13th–15th Century

View of the Pazzi Chapel in the first cloister of S. Croce

Went across the river to the Pitti Palace. The public front is massive and barren. Rooms are opulent with much of the original stuff in them, including some fantastic chests. So much work and effort went into making those rooms.

The Boboli Gardens of the palace climb the hillside behind. A grotto is included in the complex. The park is organized along a formal axis to top of the hill with many side paths, some of which lead to terraces with views of Florence. Nice day, so spent a lot of time relaxing there.

Went to Centro Di bookstore and bought a fine book with a compilation of plans and sections of ecclesiastical buildings.

Palazzo Pitti, 15th Century, Fancelli

View of the Cathedral from the Boboli Gardens

Boboli Gardens of the Palazzo Pitti

Saw the facade of Palazzo Rucellai by Alberti. It is different from other Florentine Palaces in its smooth classical order and rustication. Visited S. Spirito and enjoyed Brunelleschi's incorporation of chapels into the plan. In the end of the apse are four chapels; no one chapel is centered in the space. The altar is at the crossing, so the apse, transepts, and nave are equal in use and signification.

Saw the collection at the Uffizi. The enclosed loggias are very nice spaces with commanding views. The collection is impressive. There was a splendid collection of ink line drawings and etchings by Giorgio Morandi on display in the special gallery.

Nave of S. Spirito, 15th Century, Brunelleschi and Manetti

Facade of the Palazzo Rucellai,
15th Century, Alberti

Took a walk up to S. Miniato. The church is surrounded by a fortress wall and sits high on top of a hill with fabulous views. The siting is appropriate for this Romanesque jewel. The inlaid stonework and painted timberwork make this place glitter. Translucent marble with light seeping through is used in the apse. It is interesting that the nave and apse are decorated while the aisles are left undressed. It's a nice expression of priority. Walked from there to the Belvedere fortress on a neighboring hill with another fine view of the city.

Walked through an intense commercial belt from the Ponte Vecchio up to the cathedral area, over to S. Lorenzo, and up through the market area to my pensione. After dinner, I watched a crew shooting a film in the Piazza Signoria. They created a windy day with a giant fan and lights.

S. Miniato al Monte, 11th Century

View of Florence from S. Miniato al Monte

View from the Cathedral Dome looking towards S. Miniato in the distant hilltop

PISA

Took the train to Pisa. Beautiful day. Had a picnic lunch on the lawn around the duomo, baptistry, and tower. The facade of the cathedral was perhaps the finest element of the whole thing. The baptistry was plain inside. The docent sang harmonizing notes for us, and the reverberation time was so long that he created beautiful chords. It would make the ultimate shower stall.

Baptistery with cathedral and leaning tower

Leaning Tower of Pisa, 12th–14th Century

The town square, Piazza dei Cavalieri, was a highpoint in the town. A palace and church stand out in the square with their white plastered and frescoed surfaces glowing in the afternoon sun. Approaches seemed to focus on these facades and a statute. One approach is through the center of a building. The building acts as a triumphal arch. The view through the arch is of the statue, the palace, and church. Pisa has arcaded streets.

Nice palaces are located along the riverfront. Santa Maria della Spina is a little jewel of a chapel along the river with some beautiful carvings and many spires and projections.

Back in Florence, I climbed to the top of Brunelleschi's dome at the cathedral. Saw the inside of the double dome on the way up. Spectacular view from the top on a beautiful day.

Piazza dei Cavalieri

LUCCA

S. Giusto, 12th Century

Visited Lucca. The day's weather was rainy in the morning, sunny in the afternoon. Each walk down a street brought delightful discoveries. Many little churches and fine medieval brick palaces, some hybrids of different periods fill the town. In one place, houses are built exactly along the remains of a Roman arena with traces of Roman arches and columns in the walls. There are many towers and endless Romanesque carvings. The town is extremely rich. The Duomo S. Martino and San Michele are built similarly to the cathedral at Pisa. The town wall was made into a beautiful promenade lined with trees, wrapping the city. On a hot day, it would probably be the place to go, up high under the shade of trees catching the breezes.

S. Michele in Foro, 11th–13th Century

S. Pietro Somaldi , 12th–14th Century

Duomo S. Martino, 11th–12th Century

S. Frediano, 12th Century

S. Gulia, 13th Century

Baptismal Font, S Frediano, 12th Century

SIENA

My first major impression was the way it was built on hills. I could stand in one place facing the beginning of two streets framed by walls; one would take off downhill with a panorama of the countryside, while another one would wind steeply uphill. Tall brick or stone buildings line the narrow streets and are designed in the characteristic Gothic Italian style, which is very beautiful. Via di Citta is a major promenade in the city lined with fine 12–14th-century palaces and other buildings. The main shops are along this street. The street runs along a ridge and slopes gently up and down. For those who aren't prepared, it provides a major spatial event. As the street bends, narrow alleys play off it downhill a short distance. At the end is a lot of light. Following one of these alleys, often framed by arches above, one empties out on the Piazza del Campo with the Palazzo Pubblico and its fabulous campanile straight ahead. The Campo is a wonderful fan-shaped piazza fronted by a harmonious variety of 5- to 6-story buildings. The piazza slopes down to the palazzo. Behind the palazzo, the slope continues forming a valley. The piazza is located where the two ridges meet.

Palazzo Pubblico (13th–14th Century) in the Piazza del Campo

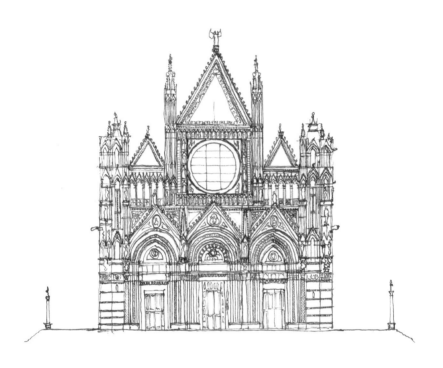

*Siena Cathedral fronting the Piazza del Duomo,
13th Century*

Top: Basilica of San Francesco, 13th–15th Centuries
Bottom: Basilica of San Domenico, 13th–14th Centuries

Saw St. Francis and St. Domenic, both similar in plan. These large barn-like churches have a nave without side aisles and are voluminous. Transepts are lined with chapels dedicated to the wealthy who helped finance the building of the church. They have nice wood trussed roofs. These churches are simple and easy to relate to.

The Siena Cathedral is a masterpiece of craftsmanship. It has inlaid floors of extreme beauty and inlaid wood in the choir seats. Nice sculpture and wall treatments. The library has fine frescos. The facade is a carnival of activity, a real delight. Lots of Germans are visiting here.

Visited Palazzo Pubblico. Beautiful frescoes and rooms. Climbed the tower for views of the city, piazza, and countryside. Visited the Pinacoteca and saw the Siena school of painting. Notable qualities include framing of scenes, rich colors, shiny gold, and depictions of cities. Buildings are colored a variety of blues, reds, and greens in abstracted forms, including towers and palaces. The buildings in the paintings take on a stage set-like quality. The evolution of these paintings is interesting and well-displayed.

Sketched. Visited Museo Opera, saw more Siena art, sculpture, and a great view of Siena from museum. Walked to the Augustinian church (classical interior), then to the opposite ridge to see S. Maria dei Servi. Had cappuccino in Piazza del Campo. Strolled Via dei Citta. Dinner.

Siena is a very pleasant city with countless vistas and many fine palaces. The architecture is earthy in color but festive in form. The geography combines with these qualities to make it an exciting place to explore. There is a lot of evidence here that Siena was once a major artistic and cultural center.

Piazza del Campo

SAN GIMIGNANO

The approach to the city was exciting. My first glimpse was a collection of stone towers on top of a hill in the distance. It was almost fairytale-like. To get to center, one passes through two layers of walls (2 gates), indicating that the city grew in rings. Buildings of stone and brick have a variety of arches. They have much layering, visible modifications, and traces of change. Brick and stone tend to blend in the walls.

Two piazzas are effectively joined by a narrow opening in the corner. They could easily have been isolated spaces if it wasn't for the architectural device used to unite them visually. The wall of the corner of the Piazza del Duomo was cut back and filled with a loggia, maintaining the volumetric quality of the piazza yet providing an opening that frames views and acts as a sort of 3-dimensional gate between the piazzas. It's not a door opening in a wall, but a connector space carved out of the building mass.

Piazza del Duomo

Piazza della Cisterna

The city is very clean. The collection of towers can be seen from city walls on top of the hill, which are part of a landscaped park. The city is not affected by modern clutter and preserves much of the medieval character. Though clearly changed and modified over the years, the changes have been subtly handled, maintaining the color of the place.

The duomo has amazing frescos. Story of St. Augustine is beautifully depicted in the choir frescoes of the Augustinian church. Returned to Siena. Last evening in this pleasant place. Had a cappuccino in the piazza this evening.

Duomo

ROME

Left Siena and arrived early afternoon in Rome. Found a hotel, took a shower, and headed for American Express. Got a bunch of letters and read them on the Spanish Steps.

Visited Borromini's S. Carlo and Bernini's S. Andrea. Both are great. S. Carlo is smaller but better than I had expected. A Trinitarian showed me around and took me up to the library in the rooms around the sanctuary. They borrow light from the sanctuary. We went up onto the roof and saw the cupola, the second floor of cloister, and the roof of the cloister.

Bernini's church is an oval shape with rich materials and color. You enter on the short axis of the oval opposite the altar. The long axis is not terminated by niches as would normally be the case. Fascinating plan.

Saw Trevi Fountain. It creates many forms of water and has many places to sit and stand around. Glimpsed at numerous other places in and around Piazza Navona. Phoned home at 11:00 pm (6:00 pm EST). Saw Capitoline Hill and Roman ruins at night.

Sanctuary, S. Carlo alle Quattro Fontane, 17th Century, Borromini

S. Carlo alle Quattro Fontane, 17th Century, Borromini
Cut away view of sanctuary and adjacent courtyard

Cupola, S. Carlo alle Quattro Fontane, 17th Century, Borromini

Dome, S. Carlo alle Quattro Fontane, 17th Century, Borromini

Courtyard, S. Carlo alle Quattro Fontane,
17th Century, Borromini

S. Andrea al Quirinale, 17th Century, Bernini

Piazza del Campidoglio, 16th Century, Michelangelo
Equestrian Statue of Marcus Aurelius, 175 AD

Saw Piazza Navona, Capitoline Hill, and the fantastic ruins of the Forum, and Palatine Hill. Saw the inside of Livia's house (House of Augustus). Three rooms are barrel vaulted with frescos superbly done in perspective. The house is quite small. I could relate to it because of what I know from the TV series I-Claudius. Saw Roma Interotta, an architecture exhibit at Trajan's Market. Saw the Pantheon.

Piazza Navona

S. Agnese in Piazza Navona, 17th Century,
Girolamo and Carlo Rainaldi

Pantheon, 25–27 BC, Agrippa

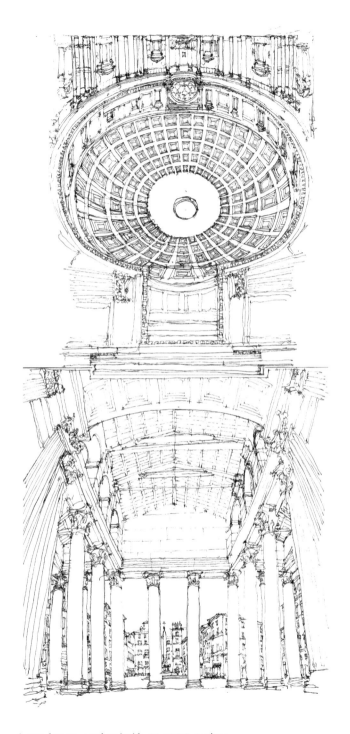

Pantheon in 180 degrees, porch to inside, 25–27 BC, Agrippa

Revisited the fabulous Trajan's Market. The market had 2–3 levels of shops. Higher levels connect to lower levels with crescent shaped ramped streets. A great barrel-vaulted space with shops is off to each side.

Trajans Market, 100–110 AD, Apollodorus of Damascus

Roman Forum

Trajans Market, 100–110 AD, Apollodorus of Damascus

Visited Coliseum. Had Lasagna. Tried to get into S. Stephano Rotunda. Saw Baths of Caracalla. Walked up by Circus Maximus and the foot of Capitoline Hill to S. Maria in Cosmedin (it was closed). Walked up Tiber, along Via Guilia, around Palazzo Faranese, up to Piazza Navona to Pantheon, to S. Ignazio, to Trevi Fountain, up via Nazionale, to S. M. Maggiore (basilica plan, fine mosaics in apse) to R. R Hotel. 10.4 km or 6.5 miles.

Colosseum, 1st Century AD

Baths of Caracalla, 3rd Century AD

Temple of Vespasian and Titus, Arch of Septimius Severus, Temple of Saturn

Arch of Constantine, 4th Century AD

Temple of Vesta, reconstruction

Curia, 44 BC

Wonderful day.

Visited Piazza S. Bernardo and S. Susanna, S. Vittoria, and the fountain. A very nice altar by Bernini is in S. Vittoria. The facades of both churches are by Carlo Maderno. The fountain celebrates entry of water into city by being placed in a triumphal arch. Walked to Villa Borghese and saw delightful eclectic architecture. The grounds are splendid with pine trees that have very tall trunks capped by needles. Walked to Porta Pia by Michelangelo. Then out to S. Costanza and S. Agnese Fuori le Mura. Costanza is a marvelous ancient mausoleum with interesting frescoes inside. Agnese is a Roman basilica plan built over St. Agnese. Went into catacombs grouped around the saint. Catacombs were, in all, a real experience.

Porto Pia, 16th Century, Michalengo

Bird House Pavilion in the Villa Borghese
Gardens, 17th Century, Girolamo Rainaldi

S. Maria della Vittoria, 17th Century,
Carlo Maderno

S. Susanna, 16th–17th Century
Carlo Maderno

S. Luca e Martina, 17th Century,
Pietro da Cortona

Chiesa Nuova, 16th Century, Martino Longhi

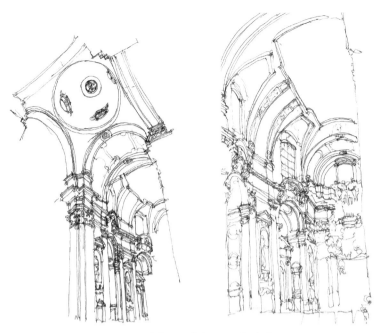

S. Mary Magdalene, 17th Century, Carlo Fontana

S. Maria Campitelli, 17th Century, Carlo Rainaldi

Went to Palazzo Barberini. The entrance sequence is very interesting. The grand salle and a set of apartments were open as an art museum. To the Spanish steps and AmEx. To Villa Giulia which has the most architectonic gardens I have seen. They create a very pleasant set of outdoor rooms. To Piazza del Popolo, down Via Ripetta to Chiesa Nuova. Got into the courtyard of the Palazzo D. Cancelleria, huge and magnificent.

Villa Gulia, 16th Century, Giacomo Vasari

Spanish Steps, 18th Century

Walked to the Villa Farnesina by Peruzzi. It was an oasis in a city full of congestion and noise. When you enter, there is a marble sarcophagus used as pool in the center of the hall. I suppose it was filled with water to refresh the visitor upon arrival at the palace. It is nice in the morning with the sun streaming into the grand salle and dining room while the loggia is in the cool refreshing shade. The villa (or palace) is one of the finest places I've been to. Of simple articulation and construction, it achieves many layers of meaning. The facade treatment corresponds to orientation and use. The river-facing wall is articulated with pilasters reinforcing the fresco in the dining room behind the wall. Its frescos are painted views of the countryside and the heavens. Upstairs the frescoes depict views of Rome and the neighboring countryside as if the walls weren't there. They are done in excellent perspective. The scale of the place is just right, unlike many palaces I've been to.

Garden Facade, Villa Farnesina, early 16th Century, Baldassare Peruzzi

Garden Loggia, Villa Farnesina

River Facing Facade, Villa Farnesina

Visited the Vatican. It's easy to tell this place has money. Visited the museum, Raphael's apartment, and the Sistine Chapel. The library had some beautiful books on display. St. Peter's Basilica was awesome, as I had expected. Bernini's canopy was particularly interesting. Went up to cupola and got a fine view of Rome. Walked to river, to Via Giulia, and saw the Farnese Palace and Spada Palace. Couldn't get inside but could get into courtyards.

At 8:00 pm, I met Prof. Patricia Waddy, and we had a big Italian dinner and good conversation at the Pantheon Trattoria. We walked to Piazza Navona along Via Vittorio Emanuel. She had just won a prize for her research and writing on the Palazzo Barberini.

St. Peter's, Vatican City, Bramante, Michelangelo, Maderno, Bernini

Baldacchin, 17th Century, Gian Lorenzo Bernini

St. Peter's Square, 17th Century, Gian Lorenzo Bernini

To Saint John the Lateran. Prominent palace next to the church. Nice mosaics are in the apse and cloister of the church. The facade has deep shadows created by portico openings.

To the baths of Caracalla. Huge, impressive ruins. Many floors sloped towards the center and could hold water for wading but were not like pools or baths with walls. They were constructed for the summer theater, which would use the baths as the stage and backdrop.

Went to the center of city and had cappuccino at a place Patricia Waddy recommended next to St. Ivo. Then I went to try the ice cream place between Pantheon and Bernini's Palazzo de Montecitorio. I had fragola (strawberry) flavor. It was the best and made from fresh fruit. To Piazza Navona, Hadrian's Tomb, Chiesa Nuova, and S. Maria in Cosmedin, Walked up to Bramante's Tempieto. It has a dramatic approach into another world. Different colors emphasize transitions. This ideal circular temple is in the center of a courtyard. It is a beautifully proportioned object.

St. John Lateran, original basilica built in the 2nd Century, revisions in the 16th Century

Tempietto, early 16th Century, Donato Bramante

ASSISI

Took a day trip to Assisi. As I arrived at the Assisi train station, the churches in the area were all ringing bells as if to greet us. Took the bus up to the town. It started to rain then and didn't stop the whole time I was there. The town is made of pink and white stone. The streets are narrow and wind up and down the hill. Churches provide anchors at each end of the town. The central square is fine, including a Roman temple front, behind of which is a church added much later.

Temple of Minerva in the Piazza del Comune

Basilica of Saint Francis of Assisi, 13th Century

S. Francesco is fascinating. It is two churches, one on top of the other, as at St. Chapelle in Paris. Different reason, though. The lower chapel is the "tomb church," the place of worship closest to the relic, St. Francis of Assisi. I believe this church was used by the clergy. It ties in easily with the monastery cloisters. The upper church is a much taller space, although its plan is very much the same. This church is accessed easily from the town. It was probably used by pilgrims and townsfolk. From a distance, the monastery looks splendidly imposing. The rhythmic arcade takes off across the landscape. It is a truly awesome site and seems to blend in with the townscape. An energetic, fun American Franciscan monk showed a group of us around.

Had a talk with an Italian soldier on the train ride back. He was very inquisitive about the U.S. He explained that all Italian men must become soldiers for a certain period of time.

FRASCATI

Visited Frascati. It was another rainy, foggy day, so the view was obscured, but you could tell that from there, the vistas to Rome and the sea must be tremendous. Later on my return trip the weather had improved and the views were spectacular until I reached the plains. The Villa Aldobrandini was splendid, as I had expected (a little larger than what I thought it would be). The garden and views were masterfully handled. Couldn't get into any other villas, but I felt I got a good sense of the Frascati villa.

Villa Aldobrandini, early 17th Century, Giacomo della Porta, Carlo Moderno, Giovanni Fontana

Garden Facade of the Villa Aldobrandini

Garden of the Villa Aldobrandini

ROME, RETURNED

Back to Rome. Visited the Castle St. Angelo, a maze of passages. Visited S. Maria de Popolo and saw splendid chapels, including the Chigi Chapel by Raphael. He brings the chapel into the side aisle simply with wall treatment extended around the chapel opening. To the Spanish Steps and then back to the hotel.

Wandered around Theatre of Marcellus and got into the art gallery at Palazzo Spada. The courtyard, perspective corridor, and facade of the palace are of great interest. Relief work inspired by Roman art is applied to the facades. Visited the huge Palazzo Farnese. Got into courtyard and backyard. The entrance corridor, a basilica plan by Sangallo, is an intense and dramatic entry. The palace was impressive.

Palazzo Spada, Baronio, Mid 16th Century, Borromini

Palazzo Farnese, Garden Facade, 16th Century, Antonio da Sangallo,

TIVOLI

Took the bus to Tivoli. Saw the Villa D'Este. The hydraulic works there are very impressive. The variety of fountains, settings, views, historical analogies, plants, etc., make this place very enjoyable. You could always hear moving water while you were in the gardens. Sometimes it would grow in intensity as you walk, and you would discover a chute or sluice or fountain you never expected to see. Lots of staged drama here. Saw a round Roman temple, beautifully sited, overlooking a gorge with a torrent of water below. Back to Rome. One final walk up the Corso to Spanish steps, one final delicious ice cream cone. Dinner near station of spaghetti, trout, lettuce, almond cake.

Villa d'Este, 16th Century

Villa d'Este, 16th Century

‹ NAPOLI ›

NAPLES

MAY 29

Because of a rail strike, I was unable to leave Rome until 2:30 pm and got into Naples at 6:30. The view of Mt. Vesuvius coming in on the train was memorable. It appears to have two peaks. Naples Centrale Station is new with a very open, platform-like design. Got a hotel for 7,000 lire/night. Walked into the old Spacca quarter. The streets are narrow and filled with activity. The shops seem to spill out on the street. The architecture is not notable, but the density of buildings obviously supports a considerable area of excitement. Occasionally, the narrow streets will open into a square which provides relief from the intense action.

Naples Waterfront

Piazza Plebiscito, 19th Century

Piazza Plebiscito, 19th Century

CAPRI

Took a hydrofoil ferry to Capri. I was immediately struck by the charm of this place. We arrived at Marina Piccola. Colorful buildings front the harbor area. Many brightly painted boats, colorful old, well-kept taxis, cafes, shops opened to the sidewalks provide a delightful introduction to Capri. Took the funicular up to the town of Capri. The island juts out of the water and has many high sheer cliffs, some forming the peaks of the island. Capri is high up, saddled between two great heights. From the town, one has splendid views of the Bay of Naples on one side and the Tyrrhenian Sea on the other side. The combination of colorful, action-packed streets, gardens of flowers, and a tremendous variety of other vegetation, geography affording spectacular views, luxurious hotels, and bars gives this place an intoxicating atmosphere. I must come here to stay someday.

Capri Waterfront

Capri

Capri Waterfront

View from Anacapri

Took a bus to Anacapri, located even higher, with panoramas of Capri, the harbor, and the bay of Naples all at once. The Villa San Michele was well worth the visit. The views were best from there, and the air in the luxuriant gardens had the scent of flowers and pine trees. This visit heightened my senses. Walked up to Tiberius' villa and walked in his loggia at the extreme end of the island facing the bay at the edge of a sheer cliff. Even 2,000 years later, I agree with him that Capri is a good hangout. Had pizza, local white wine called Tiberio, gin and tonic, cappuccino. It was easy to spend money there. On the ferry back, I met an American and Australian. Had a nice talk, and we had fun trying to communicate with a bunch of Italians. Overall, it was a wonderful day with splendid weather.

Villa San Michele

POMPEII

Took the train to Pompeii. Was greeted by taxi drivers who told me it was far away from the station. I walked there in 10 minutes. First saw the well-preserved amphitheater. A large lawn surrounded by a loggia or stoa in front of the amphitheater was used for a training ground. Walked on Roman streets. Sidewalks are a foot above street level at minimum. Stepping stones make it easier to cross the streets. Cartwheels would pass between the stones. You could see the ruts caused by the cartwheels. Saw the cemetery with mausoleums that rival those at cemeteries back home. Saw casts of Romans caught by the lava and frozen for the rest of time in their odd positions at the moment of death. The casts of a family were particularly moving, the mother shielding the child and the father a couple of feet away, supporting himself on his elbows looking at his family. The bones and skulls of the Romans have been well preserved. In the cast, one can see the lines of clothes, sandals, hair, etc.

Pompeii Amphitheater

Pompeii Street

Roman Villa Atrium

Saw many shops fronting streets with villas behind. Frescos and mosaics in many have been preserved. They are reconstructing the roofs of some of the villas, and so I got a feel for the quality of spaces in these luxurious Roman villas. The roof shields the sun creating cool pleasant spaces, different from the hot, dusty streets. The basins were exquisitely made with white marble. The gardens were lush. Essentially all the spaces were "outside" in that they were not completely sealed from the outside, yet the progression of spaces, vestibulum, atrium, peristyle with the "rooms" tablinum and triclinium, provided the necessary degrees of privacy. The spaces of the villas are inward-looking, walls and shops shielding them from the outside. The only door that I remember was the door to the house. Very pleasant, livable places.

Saw the forum with its various markets, temples, basilicas, pedestals for statuary. Always while looking at these places loomed Vesuvius in the background, now much taller than it was when Pompeii flourished.

Roman Villa Garden

PAESTUM

Took the train to Paestum and experienced my first real Greek temples, sited on a flat plain between the sea and the mountain ranges. It was very nice to sit up in them, between massive solid columns in the sunlight with the steady sea breezes. One gets a certain feeling of timelessness or permanence. Very ennobling structures. The stone colors of the temples are slightly different. A considerable number of Greek ruins reveal a town that stretched from the temples and include remains of an amphitheater facing the mountains.

Second Temple of Hera II, 460–450 BC (Formerly believed to be dedicated to Poseidon)

First Temple of Hera, 550 BC

Second Temple of Hera II, 460–450 BC

The Hera Temples

A few notes about the Italians of the south. They seem very open and less reserved than the Italians in the north. I have had quite a few speak to me on the streets. There were two incidents in which groups of teenage girls barraged me with questions wanting pictures taken. All very nice and fun. In Naples, I saw a woman store owner chase after a bunch of kids with a stick. One Italian gentleman waved and greeted me as if we were good friends. He was curious about what I was doing. Again, very friendly, and gregarious, even to complete strangers.

Left Naples at 20:00 on a night train bound for Palermo. Shared a cabin with three other Italians. They loaded the train on a ferry boat at Villa S. Giovanni for short ride to Messina. I don't know why they just don't build a bridge. The ferry was nice. Stood beneath the bridge of the ship and watched the action (around 3:00 am). Saw some of Sicilian coast before arriving in Palermo at 8:30.

PALERMO

JUNE 2

Found hotel for 4,000 lire a night. Saw the beautiful San Giovanni degli Eremiti. Pink domes. Arab-Norman. Saw the Palatine Chapel with its dazzling mosaics depicting the stories of the Old Testament. The Moorish ceiling was great (just like what they have in Spain). King Roger would sit at back of nave on a throne during mass. Geometric mosaics are on the floor and everywhere. Slept during siesta. Saw the town center. Colorful piazzas are made so by the pink and yellow walls of palaces. Santa Maria dell'Ammiraglio had more great mosaics in it. I like the way the corners of the arches and vaults are rounded (tapered) rather than sharp edges. It gives the mosaics a sort of soft blanket effect, very smooth, like rich garments. It's hard to think of more fabulous insides than these mosaic spaces with their fine vaulting. San Cataldo is much like S. Giovanni, pink domes, and well-proportioned solid masonry. San Cataldo had the original mosaic floors and very fine delicate bas-relief along the cornice line on the outside. The box shape with pink domes and a simple plan are very nice.

San Giovanni degli Eremiti, 12th Century

San Giovanni degli Eremiti, cloister of the 6th Century Benedictine monastery

San Cataldo Domes

San Cataldo, 12th Century

Palermo Cathedral

Piazza Pretoria

MONREALE

Took the bus to Monreale. Traveled up a broad valley and climbed one side to a shelf, Monreale. The cathedral was the primary objective. It has unbelievable mosaics in it. Not only picture mosaics of the bible but patterns and designs of infinite variety adorn the floors and walls. The geometric patterns using a few piece types are varied and intricate. Saw the courtyard planted with flowers. Columns are composed of variety of shafts carved and decorated with mosaics in many patterns and capitals, very freely executed using organic forms, human forms, scenes, and stories, or just abstract designs. Yet all the capitals conform to basic dimensional and proportional guidelines. Their variety within these guidelines is astonishing.

Monreale and the Cathedral, 12th–13th Century

CEFALÙ

Took the train to Cefalù. Walked through town, down along the harbor, up to the piazza. Had a beer. Then walked up behind the cathedral and up the face of the cliff to the foot of the sheer wall. Cefalù is sited on a jut of land that slopes up from the sea to a cliff of tremendous size. Approaching Cefalù by rail from Palermo, one is impressed by its siting and the cathedral, which towers above the town but is dwarfed by the cliff right next to it. At the foot of the cliff wall, I was already above the towers of the cathedral, and there obtained a splendid panorama of Cefalù and the Sicilian coast. Visited the cathedral (being restored at the time). More fine mosaics in the apse and choir.

Returned to Palermo. Had dinner for 3300 lire ala carte (prices cheap down here). Strolled up the Ruggero Settimo, a tree-lined boulevard with modern buildings, fine shops and restaurants, and corporate headquarters. Palermo is no backwoods town. They have a very elegant quarter here. Had another delicious pastry.

6-3-78

Cathedral of Cefalù, 12th–13th Century

City of Cefalù on the Tyrrhenian Coast

SEGESTA

Took a train to Segesta and saw a fine Doric temple. The problem was that it was fenced off, and you couldn't get in. There was one attendant at the station but no one else. The station, built to house a bar, was abandoned. Only the sounds of insects and the hot sun. Desolation. Walked up to the ruins, then two tour buses and a bunch of noisy tourists arrived. End desolation.

Took train on to Trapani but couldn't get to Erice, so back to Palermo. Saw fine sandy beaches on way back. Walked to Palermo's harbor and along shoreline. Carnival and lots of people this relaxing Sunday afternoon.

Segesta, Doric Temple, 420s BC

Segesta, Doric Temple, 420s BC

AGRIGENTO

Took the train to Agrigento, passing through the central part of Sicily. The landscape is beautiful, rolling sometimes jagged hills covered with grass, vines, and cactus. Herds of sheep roam the hillsides. It is sparsely populated. Approaching from the inland side, Agrigento is an impressive modern hill town stretched along a ridge. This is one of the rare times modern apartment blocks seem to be clustered and organized nicely. Agrigento has a nice tree-lined boulevard, one side lined with buildings and the other along the edge of a cliff with a tremendous view of the temples and Mediterranean. The temples Juno and Concord are sited on top of small hills with spectacular views from each of Agrigento on the ridge to the north and the Mediterranean to the south. It's nice being up in them on a sunny afternoon, being cooled by the breezes coming from the vast sea. These are impressive yellow stoned Doric temples. Juno is right along the edge of a cliff. Both are along the same ridge. Saw some other ruins. Saw a Greek bouleuterion with a gentle sloping audience. The slope was not steep enough to seat people on steps, so they made stone benches. Met some Italians on the train back to Palermo who gave me some suggestions of things to see.

Temple of Concordia

Temple of Concordia

Temple of Hera

Greek Bouleuterion

SYRACUSE

Took a train to Syracuse, passing through the heart of Sicily. Rugged country tempered by vegetation. Soft rolling wheat fields in one area. Oil docks and refineries at Augusta, just outside Syracuse. Was stared at a lot because of my American t-shirt, shorts, boots, Philmont belt, camera, and luggage, quite a contrast to the normal Italian—tight-fitting knit pants or blue jeans, tight-fitting sports shirt, shiny shoes, neat hair. Visited a Greek and Roman site and Roman arena. Walked to the old town. Nice harbor and waterfront. Big promenades along the water. The cathedral was most unusual. It was constructed on a ruined Greek temple. Some of the columns had remained standing and were filled in between to create walls. The nave walls were the walls of the temple shrine rooms. The facade was Baroque, added onto the front of the building. The "pilasters," instead of being inspired by antiquity, were antiquity.

Roman Arena

Cathedral of Syracuse, originally the 5th Century BC Temple of Athena

143

TAORMINA

Visited a Greek amphitheater beautifully sited overlooking Syracuse and the bay. Then took the train to Taormina, a city sited on a balcony overlooking the sea with an extension along the ridge of the peninsula. A Greek theater is located on that ridge and is one of the most spectacular siting jobs I've seen. Along the top of the theater, you can look out beyond and down the coast for miles or straight ahead to the stage with the bay and Mount Etna in the distance. The Romans added a stage set to the theater. The main street in town with nice shops and cafes adds a commercial appeal that make it popular to visit.

Taormina

Taormina, Amphitheater

MESSINA

Left Syracuse on a train bound for Rome. Saw Mt. Etna emitting smoke as the train passed by. For quite a while, that mountain fills your window's view and doesn't seem to move as the train speeds on. It is truly a huge mountain. To Messina marina, left Sicily on a ferry boat at noon. The boat trip to Villa S. Giovanni on the rich blue harbor was memorable. Took a train to Reggio Calabria. Then at 4:30 caught a train to Bari. For most of the trip, we passed by stunning beaches. The surf wasn't big, but they seemed to have everything else. Got into Bari at midnight. Staying in Hotel Roma.

Messina

ALBEROBELLO

Took an FSE train for a day trip to Alberobello. A large section of the town and the countryside around is built of "trullis," stone buildings with stone conical roofs, delightful fairytale-like houses with whitewashed walls. Inside, the spaces are vaulted in stone. Some interiors are whitewashed too. Niches are sometimes made for beds. Children sleep in lofts. They have smooth stone floors and are very cool and comfortable on this hot sunny day. Seemed to be adequate light in them, but who wants bright spaces inside anyways when it's so bright outside. The roof is comprised of two layers of stone; vaulting stone, and sheathing stone. A little gable in the wall is often made for the front door. Sometimes the roofs would seem to merge. The streets in the town were well-kept, built for the pedestrian. Entrance doors are often just beads hanging in the doorway. Saw couple of people whitewashing their walls. They were very attentive to the building they live in.

Trulli Houses in Alberobello

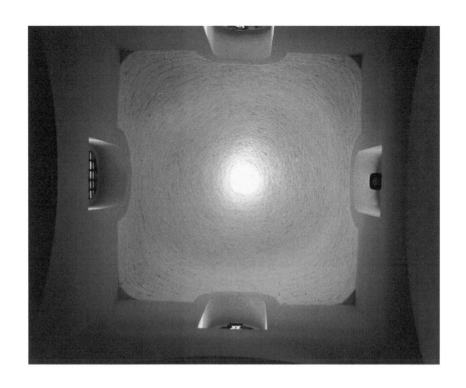

Trulli Houses in Alberobello

Trulli Houses in Alberobello

URBINO

Left Bari at 9:00 for Urbino. Long train ride up the coast. I had a compartment all to myself. Lots of beautiful beaches along the Adriatic coast. Stopped at Fano and caught the commuter train to Urbino. Took a bus with all my luggage up into the Piazza Republica. I was lucky to find a hotel right away. For 5000 lire it is one of the nicest places I've stayed in. New furnishings and nicely finished interiors within an old Urbino palace. My window looks down into the courtyard and out to roofscapes and the tower of S. Francesco. Walked around town. Saw piazzas around the Palazzo Ducale, brick buildings, and streets of a quality comparable to the infrastructure of Siena. Saw some of DeCarlo's additions to the town from outside but could not get inside them. His modern university buildings blend in beautifully with the infrastructure of the old city.

Visited Palazzo Ducale. A most incredible room is to be found inside this Renaissance palace. The walls are paneling made of inlaid wood depicting scenes in perspective. Incredible craftsmanship. The palace facades, courtyard, and spaces are wonderful.

Inspected DeCarlo's work again. His education building presents brick walls to the streets, with occasional openings. The brick is handled like the older buildings. These walls work so well with the immediate surroundings and the typologies of this section of the town. (i.e., terraced gardens, retaining walls, etc.) Large academic spaces are brilliantly inserted into the delicate urban fabric.

Walked down a ramp to the Mercantile Plaza. Two layers of parking are underneath the plaza. Walked on over to DeCarlo's famous dorms on the hillside. This building comfortably blends into the landscape with tremendous view, especially from the center building. I found the paths and center building at first to be maze-like. I could never quite tie everything together in my head. But I wonder if it's necessary to or even desirable in a building like this. This dorm is treated like a hill town such as Urbino; a maze of streets going up and down but always seeming to eventually lead to the center. Much new construction was going on there using the same materials as the original 1960s dorm. The physical fabric of this university is expanding tremendously.

Visited Raphael's house, a pleasant Urbino residence. Entered and climbed to the prima piano. Towards the back on this level is the courtyard (instead of at entrance level) due to the hillside landscape. Very comfortable intimate palace type.

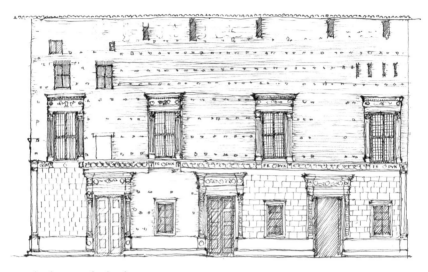

Ducal Palace Facade Sketch

Ducal Palace, 15th Century in Piazza Pascoli

Ducal Palace Courtyard

Student Housing, University of Urbino, 20th Century, Giancarlo DeCarlo

Returned to DeCarlo's education building. It was open, and I went inside. Fine detailing and finishes. Lots of natural light even penetrating down to the floor level of the congress hall. The round courtyard and curved wall of the congress hall facilitate an easy meandering circulation. It is very easy to flow in that building. Squares wouldn't have done it. The easy free assembly of spaces and objects, positive and negative, can be compared to Urbino itself. In fact, the assembly of the primary functions—work, living, circulation, and leisure in terms of spatial organization and placement with relation to context and external influences is handled much like the complex juxtaposition of these functions in Urbino. Besides all that, the spaces felt nice. The flexible assembly hall and skylight combination was particularly notable.

Walked out to DeCarlo's new housing and art school. Not sure what to think about the housing. Really huge objects on the landscape. The art school was under construction. One section of the terraced concrete levels was without the roof, and the one next to it had the roof. An interesting comparison. DeCarlo's two major nodes of external influence on the old city seem to be logically placed as attractions for future growth. They are along two major points of access into the town.

Strolled the city at night. Got a fine view of the palace, mercantile ramp, and duomo from an opposite hill near a fortress. Urbino is an exciting city and much of the life of it comes from the vast student population that inhabits and gathers in places like the Piazza Republica in the evenings.

Urbino University education building, congress hall

Urbino University education building street facade on the left

Urbino University education building roof terrace with skylight over the congress hall

RAVENNA

Left Urbino in the morning. Took a local train to Ressaro and from there caught a train to Ravenna. Cloudy day. Went directly to S. Vitale. Mosaics in the presbytery and apse are rich and colorful. Recognized the Empress Theodora and Emperor Justinian posed with their courts, forever watching the activities. Mosaics depict their elaborate lifestyle. Overall, though, the church wasn't quite what I had expected. The round campanile nearby is characteristic of Ravenna. Unfortunately, the Tomb of Galla Placidia was filled up with scaffolding, but I was still able to see some of the mosaics, very rich in color and in glorious contrast to the rough brick exterior. There is something marvelous about the contrast between the simple rough, primary yet well-proportioned exterior and a smooth plastic, glittering, colorful interior such as you find in this tomb. The mosaics are well preserved. This inside-outside relationship that one experiences heightens the mystery of the sarcophagus inside the tomb. Again, the exterior similar in nature to the tomb's exterior is presented, but what does the inside look like? Drama.

Baptistery of Ortodossi, 5th Century

S Vitale, 6th Century

Tomb of Galla Placidia, 425–450 AD

From the tomb, I walked to the Baptistery degli Ortodossi, more rich mosaics. The baptism of Christ is the subject of the mosaic in the dome, a logical theme for pictorial representation. The colors are dazzling. The power of the central plan is reinforced by the design of interior surface treatment, and together a universal space is created.

Visited Dante's tomb and the fine Basilica of San Francesco. The mosaic floor of the crypt is underwater. So is the excavated floor area in S. Vitale. The seawater level must just be a few feet below ground level here. Visited St. Apollinare Nuovo. Large mosaics of processions create an interesting overall design effect in the nave. The Arian Baptistry was another centrally planned building, smaller than the other baptistry. Only the ceiling is mosaiced here, but the inside-outside effect is great. It's almost like walking into a mysterious box and looking up into another world.

Basilica of San Francesco, 9th–10th Centuries

Basilica of Sant'Apollinare Nuovo, 6th Century

Took the bus out to St. Apollinaris in Classe. Large fine basilica with gorgeous mosaics in the apse. It's very bright in these churches with interesting sarcophagi placed in the aisles. I can relate to these churches.

S. Appollinaris in Classe, 6th Century

Apse of S. Apollinare in Classe

FERRARA

Left Ravenna for Ferrara. Walked from the station up past the stadium in the old section. Walked around the Chateau d'Este, over to the duomo. The Cathedral of Ferrara is a fabulous Romanesque building in a sort of Pisan style with a wide elevation. The side elevation faces a large piazza, and a shopping arcade is incorporated into it. Pink and white stone and brick are the materials. It has a variety of capitals, and in the upper part of the long elevation double columns sometimes spiral or wrap around each other, a real treat. Nice piazza. There are two pedestals, one a flunky column, support statues and flank a large portal in front of the duomo and help signal the entrance into the principal civic building from many directions.

Walked over to the Diamanti Palace, which is the city's principal art museum. I was the only one there, and a gentleman who restores paintings gave me a personal tour. The art work there includes paintings on metal surfaces, wood, and canvas. The wood was often deteriorated by insects. We had trouble communicating because of the language barrier, but he was able to get across some basic ideas. He showed me the areas on the paintings that had been repainted or "restored" in the past. One foot of Christ was repainted with six toes instead of five. Really lousy old restorations with poor color matching, etc. He then took me into his workshop, where he was working on the paintings removing the old restoration work by scraping and wiping with chemicals. Really interesting and lots of work to do.

Explored the city and saw many fine brick buildings and some nice palaces in a rather extensive old section. Much of the old character of Ferrara is still there. An interesting arcaded shopping street is near the duomo.

Palazzo Dei Diamanti, 14th–15th Century

Palazzo Schifanoia, 15th Century

Went inside the Castle Estense. Some nice frescos in there. Saw a large exhibit of ancient pottery and small household objects, Greek 3–4 cent. BC. Nice shapes to the pots and plates. Colorful small bottles. The Palazzo Costabili is a nice palace with two sides of a beautiful courtyard completed and a huge grand salle. It was raining, so I decided to leave Ferrara and arrived in Venice. Found a room for 10,000 lire at the Hotel Union. Went to Piazza S. Marco (sun shining then). Got a letter from home at Am Ex. Walked to the Rialto bridge area. Ate.

Duomo of Ferrara, 12th Century, Campanile, 15th Century attributed to Alberti

166

Palazzo Costabili, 16th Century

Palazzo Costabili, 16th Century

VENICE

JUNE 16

Cashed traveler's checks. Sketched two palaces along grand canal. Saw a nice collection of modern art at the Peggy Guggenheim Foundation. I enjoyed work by Klee, Braque, Ozenfant, Picasso, Ernst, Mondrian, Kandinsky a constructivist. Got my hair cut. Tried to sketch some more, but it rained. Bought newspaper and ate dinner. Went to a concert at St. Simone Piccolo featuring flute and piano music by Vivaldi.

Palazzo Loredan dell'Ambasciatore

Venetian Facades

Palazzo Pisani Moretta

To Ca Pesaro, which houses the International Gallery of Modern Art. Saw a nice series of views of Venice by Guarini. Many Italian painters represented, plus works by Kandinsky, Matisse, Klee, and other notables.

Walked to Campo S. Paulo and then to Campo dei Frari. Saw a fantastic painting of the "Assumption of the Virgin" in the altar of dei Frari by Titian. The composition and colors are great. Other notable works are there. The frescoed spaces of Scuola di S. Rocco are overwhelming. It was quite an undertaking done by a school of artists. To Rialto and tried to sketch, but it rained. Window-shopped my way to S. Marco.

Went inside S. Marco for more study. Visited the treasury, which contains some of the most incredible craftsmanship of objects in gold, jewels, and enamels. Delicacy beyond belief. Saw a glittering altar screen done in gold. It's on a pivot so that it can be hidden from the view of the nave. Nice marble and travertine canopy is over the altar. Got down into the crypt then up to museum, which is adjacent to the loggia on the facade of the church, from which you can get great views of S. Mark's Square. Walked along the catwalks of the nave and aisle crossings for close inspection of the mosaics. Then to Harry's Bar for a gin and tonic. Then dinner.

St. Mark's Square

To Academy Gallery to see a collection of Venetian painting. It's laid out to show chronologically the development of the school and its outside influences. It is a very pleasant gallery with delightful works to see. The earliest works are influenced by mosaics. They have gold backgrounds like the mosaics at St. Marks, but gradually over time these disappear. Did some sketches. Lunch in S. Luca Square. Wandered up past Rialto Bridge to S. M. dei Miracoli, a beautifully done stone church with the appearance of the Pisan school in the application of stone colors on the outside. To S. Giovanni e Paolo then over to S. Francesco dei Vigna and the naval base. Walked down along Bacino San Marco and saw lots of activity on the water. A big cruise ship moved in there. Back to S. Marco Square and stepped into the church for a minute. Had coffee at the Caffe Florian then dinner. In the evening, I went back to S. Giovanni e Paolo to see the Hurricane Choir from somewhere in Arkansas perform American spiritual music. It was a pleasant concert. This large gothic church has no buttressing but is held together by iron tie rods and beams.

S. Francesco dei Vigna, 16th Century
Facade by Palladio

S. M. dei Miracoli, 15th Century

Went to San Giorgio Maggiore and Il Redentore, both by Palladio. The facades glimmer and are easily seen by throngs of tourists. The spaces inside are sort of surrealistic. They provide an interesting contrast in their forms, elements, and colors to an already pleasant Venice. Il Redentore's spaces are subdivided, the nave from the choir, by columns and entablatures spatially reinforced by the vaulting. The light is also different in each.

I attended a very pleasant flute and guitar concert at the Ca'Rezzonico, sitting in the grand Salle (the great central hall common to the typical Venetian palace) among beautiful paintings. This is also an art museum. The view from the balconies of the Grand Canal was impressive.

S. Giorgio Maggiore, 16th Century, Andrea Palladio

Il Redentore Sketches, 16th Century, Andrea Palladio

PADOVA

Took a quick trip from Venice to Padova. It is a rather large prosperous city. Visited the Basilica del Santo, a very large voluminous basilica covered by domes. It seems to have been influenced by St. Marks however it has plain walls and vaults, unlike St. Marks. There were lots of pilgrims there passing by the relics blowing kisses and crossing themselves, and attending services, two or three running simultaneously. It has nice courtyards. Up to Palazzo della Ragione, a marvelous, arcaded structure in the center of the piazza. The ground level was three or four interior pedestrian shopping streets full of market shops and a huge space above that was covered with a large wooden roof. An art exhibit was being held in this space, and there was a curious huge wooden horse there too. This building, simple in its idea, is both functional and beautiful. Saw Chiesa degli Eremitani, which has a nice keel-type wooden roof ceiling thing and saw Cappella Scrovegni. The inside is covered with frescos by Giotto that show views of Christian stories and are painted architectural elements. The walls are quite flat, yet the frescos make it seem less obvious that they are.

Basilica del Santo, 13th Century

Palazzo della Ragione, 13th–14th Century

VICENZA

Left Venice and arrived at Vicenza. Deposited baggage and walked down the Via Palladio to the Palazzo Chiericati, which is being used as the city's art museum. I bought Ackerman's study of Palladio and read his chapter on Palladio's civic and palace work and his study of Palladio's theory as guides to the work I saw that day in Vicenza. It enriched my visit and made it memorable. His observations both heightened and confirmed my awareness of things. Also bought a book with photographs of models done of Palladio's projects.

Left Vicenza and arrived at Verona, the last city on my Italian tour, as it was the first Italian city I visited a few years ago. My impressions of it have not changed. Reddish-rich colors. Active pedestrian streets, fine shops, piazzas, and palaces. Had dinner in Piazza dei Signore and tried excellent local wine.

Palazzo Chiericati, 16th Century, Andrea Palladio

Palazzo Chiericati courtyard

Teatro Olimpico, 16th Century, Palladio and Scamozzi

Palazzo Chiericati, 16th Century, Andrea Palladio

Basilica Palladiana, 16th Century, Andrea Palladio

Palazzo del Capitaniato, 16th Century, Andrea Palladio

Palazzo Valmarana, 16th Century, Andrea Palladio

Villa Rotunda, 16th Century, Andrea Palladio

Palazzo Barbaran da Porto, 16th Century, Andrea Palladio

Palazzo Porto, 16th Century, Andrea Palladio

VERONA

JUNE 21

Saw St. Zeno's again; much darker inside because the weather was cloudy with rain. It is a fine Romanesque church with a raised choir and huge crypt. It has an interesting door. Went to the Pinacoteca in the Castelvecchio. It was very interesting, not just because of the paintings, but because the museum is in an old fortress. I wandered through town center and lunched next to their Roman amphitheater, then to the railroad station.

Caught 16:34 train for Copenhagen to see my Danish family. Farewell Italy. Shortly after leaving Verona, we hit the gorgeous rugged southern Alps. Blue sky, setting sun, jagged peaks. Had a dinner of pasta, veal, vegetables, rolls, and caffe in the dining car while enjoying the fabulous views.

Basilica of San Zeno cloister

Amphitheater, 30 AD

Basilica of San Zeno, 10th–14th Century

5-13-78

CONCLUSION

During my career as an architect and urban designer, I was able to draw on lessons learned visiting places in Italy that spring and early summer of 1978. My travel experiences contributed to an understanding of the role of architecture in the creation of beautiful cities and the richness given to a work by teams of inspired patrons and talented designers and artists. My trip was a blessing and luxury, a period of education that, in hindsight, was essential. Book learning and classroom study of important places can only get you so far. It is essential to travel and see these places to understand and learn from them more fully.

PAUL OSTERGAARD, FAIA is a Consulting Principal for Urban Design Associates and an instructor in the School of Architecture at Carnegie-Mellon University. He has helped his clients create mixed-income neighborhoods, revitalized downtowns, new urban centers, transit-oriented districts, and new communities. His projects in North America, Europe, and the Middle East have a solid foundation in urban design principles and values but with a wide range of place-based design responses. He enjoys introducing young professionals to the practice of urban design.

Then

Now

Printed in the USA
CPSIA information can be obtained
at www.ICGtesting.com
LVHW070455020923
756999LV00006B/30